Bugs that Bite

Ticks

By Simon Rose

www.av2books.com

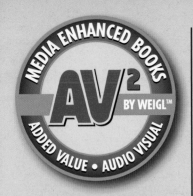

AV² provides enriched content that supplements and complements this book. Weigl's AV² books strive to create inspired learning and engage young minds in a total learning experience.

Your AV² Media Enhanced books come alive with...

Audio
Listen to sections of the book read aloud.

Key Words
Study vocabulary, and complete a matching word activity.

Go to **www.av2books.com**, and enter this book's unique code.

Video
Watch informative video clips.

Quizzes
Test your knowledge.

BOOK CODE

S 3 1 5 5 1 5

Embedded Weblinks
Gain additional information for research.

Slide Show
View images and captions, and prepare a presentation.

AV² by Weigl brings you media enhanced books that support active learning.

Try This!
Complete activities and hands-on experiments.

... and much, much more!

Published by AV² by Weigl
350 5ᵗʰ Avenue, 59ᵗʰ Floor
New York, NY 10118
Websites: www.av2books.com   www.weigl.com

Copyright © 2015 AV² by Weigl
All rights reserved. No part of this publication may be reproduced, stored in a retrieval system, or transmitted in any form or by any means, electronic, mechanical, photocopying, recording, or otherwise, without the prior written permission of the publisher.

Library of Congress Control Number: 2013953048
ISBN 978-1-4896-0778-2 (hardcover)
ISBN 978-1-4896-0779-9 (softcover)
ISBN 978-1-4896-0780-5 (single user eBook)
ISBN 978-1-4896-0781-2 (multi-user eBook)

Printed in the United States of America in North Mankato, Minnesota
1 2 3 4 5 6 7 8 9 0   18 17 16 15 14

012014
WEP301113

Senior Editor Aaron Carr
Art Director Terry Paulhus

Photo Credits
Every reasonable effort has been made to trace ownership and to obtain permission to reprint copyright material. The publishers would be pleased to have any errors or omissions brought to their attention so that they may be corrected in subsequent printings.

Weigl acknowledges Getty Images as its primary image supplier for this title.
Page 7: Mat Pound-USDA Agricultural Research Service Country-United States.

Bugs that Bite

Ticks

Meet the Tick

Ticks are tiny creatures. Most **species** are only 0.6 inches (15 millimeters) long. They are more closely related to spiders and scorpions than to insects.

There are many different types of ticks. They are found all over the world. Wherever they live, ticks have one thing in common. They all feed on the blood of other creatures.

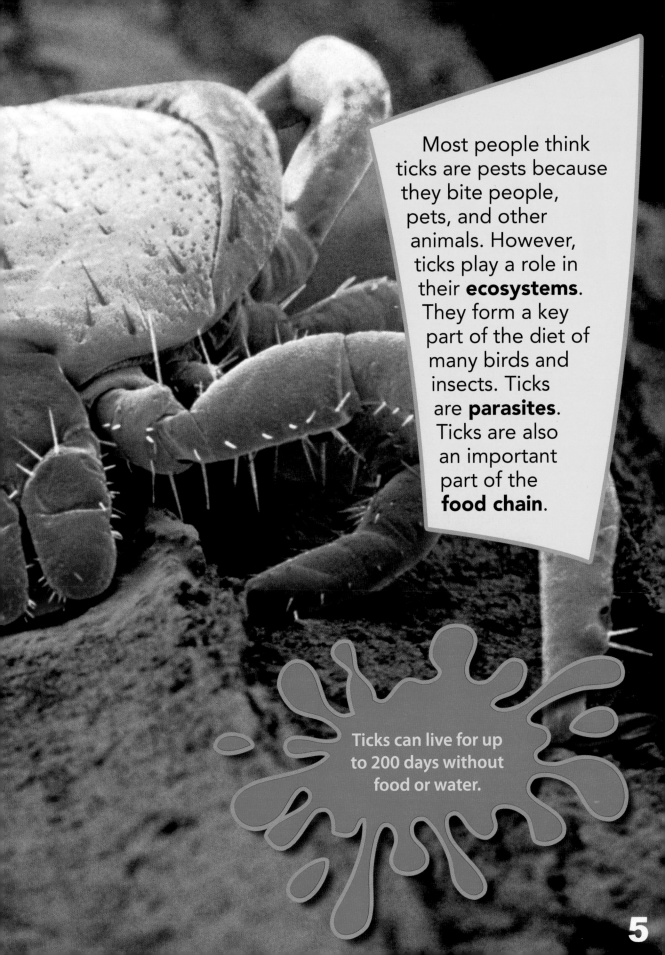

Most people think ticks are pests because they bite people, pets, and other animals. However, ticks play a role in their **ecosystems**. They form a key part of the diet of many birds and insects. Ticks are **parasites**. Ticks are also an important part of the **food chain**.

Ticks can live for up to 200 days without food or water.

All About Ticks

There are more than 800 species of ticks. They are classified into three groups. The groups are Ixodids, Argasids, and Nuttalliellidae. Ixodids are hard ticks. Argasids are soft ticks. Nuttalliella is a separate species. This species is found only in southern Africa.

Ticks do not fly or jump, but they have very good senses. Ticks can sense an animal's breath, body odors, and body heat. They can also sense an animal's movements. When an animal is near, the tick climbs onto it. Next, the tick attaches itself to the **host** animal's skin. The tick then begins to feed on the blood of its host. Depending on the species, a tick may live for only two months or as long as two years.

There are about 100 species of ticks in the United States.

Types of Ticks

Ixodids

- Have about 700 species worldwide
- Have a hard shell called a **scutum**
- Have a prominent head that projects outward from the body

Argasids

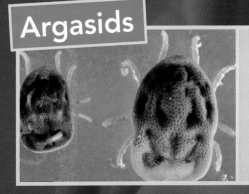

- Have about 200 species worldwide
- Are usually found on birds
- Do not have a hard shell

Nuttalliella

- Made up of only one species
- Found only in southern Africa
- Females have features of both hard and soft ticks

Tick Habitats

Ticks live in every region of the world, but they are more common in countries that have warm, humid climates. Ticks prefer these **habitats** because they need moisture in the air. Moisture is necessary for their **metamorphosis**. This is the process by which a tick develops into an adult.

While waiting for a host to pass by, or in between feedings, adult ticks rest on grasses and other plant life native to their **habitat**.

Ticks also need to live where there are enough host animals. Host animals can live in forests, in the countryside, or on farms. Wherever hosts are found, ticks can be present as well. In tropical countries, ticks are often found on farm animals. The deer tick is also called the blacklegged tick. It is found in the eastern and northern midwestern regions of the United States. It is also found in parts of Canada. These ticks usually live in the same areas as deer. These can be places with sandy soil, hardwood trees, and rivers or streams.

After a tick has fed on the blood of its host, its body becomes enlarged and round.

Tick
Features

MOUTH

A tick uses its mouthparts to pierce the host's skin and obtain its blood. The mouthparts include two **palps** and two **chelicerae**. The palps move out of the way during feeding. The chelicerae cut through the host's skin. The mouth also has a barbed, needlelike feeding tube. This tube is called a hypostome. The hypostome is inserted into the skin, and its barbs help the tick stay attached to the host.

HEAD

The hard tick has a head and mouthparts that project outward from the body. In a soft tick, the head is hidden under the body.

HALLERS ORGAN

The front section of the tick's front legs contains a sensory organ called Haller's Organ. This organ can sense changes in temperature, air movements, and humidity. This organ can also sense a host's breath, odors, and movement.

BODY

The tick's body is divided into two sections. The **capitulum** includes the tick's head and mouthparts. The **idiosoma** includes the tick's legs, digestive stem, and reproductive organs.

LEGS

Ticks have eight legs with six sections on each leg. The leg sections are called the coxa, trochanter, femur, tibia, pretarsus, and tarsus. Short, spiny hairs cover each leg, and each leg ends in a tiny claw. The claws and hairs help a tick grab on to vegetation and on to its host. A tick can fold its legs against its body when it is not moving.

Tick Life Cycle

Most ticks go through four life stages. These are egg, larva, **nymph**, and adult. After the female tick has mated, she lays her eggs. When the eggs have hatched, ticks must eat blood at every stage of their life cycle. Without blood, they will not grow or develop.

Stage 1
Egg

A tick begins its life as an egg. The female hard tick attaches itself to a host before mating. Once on the host, she begins to eat, sometimes for more than 24 hours straight. The female dies after laying up to 18,000 eggs. The male hard tick dies after mating. Soft ticks do not eat as much blood at one time. They will lay eggs on more than one occasion.

The female tick waits patiently for a host to come by. She will soon eat and then lay her eggs.

Stage 2
Larva

When an egg hatches, a larva emerges. The larva has only six legs. Otherwise, it looks like an adult tick. The larva must find a host right away. Without a host, the larva cannot grow. The first host is usually a lizard or a small mammal. After the larva has eaten enough blood, it leaves the host. Its growth has begun.

Stage 3
Nymph

Between one and three weeks later, the larva **molts** and becomes a nymph. The nymph has eight legs. It finds another host, most often a bird, a small mammal, or a lizard. After feeding, the nymph leaves the host and continues to develop. Some soft tick nymphs molt more than once, finding a new host each time. After molting for the last time, the tick becomes an adult.

Stage 4
Adult

Adult ticks usually live for only a few days, but some species live for several months. All ticks need to find a host quickly or they will not survive. Ticks often feed on specific types of host animals during different stages of their life cycle. Once the female tick has eaten and is ready to mate, the life cycle begins again.

How Do Ticks Bite?

Ticks wait on the tips of leaves or grasses when they are looking for a host. This is called questing. When an animal brushes by, the tick climbs onto the animal's body.

After a tick has anchored itself, it must pierce the host's skin. Once that is done, the tick is ready to dive in and feast on the host's blood.

Once a tick has found a place to feed, it cuts into the animal's skin with its chelicerae. The tick then inserts its feeding tube. In some species, the feeding tube has barbs to hold the tick in place while it feeds. Ticks also inject special saliva into the host. This prevents the animal from feeling that the tick is attached.

Piercing the Skin

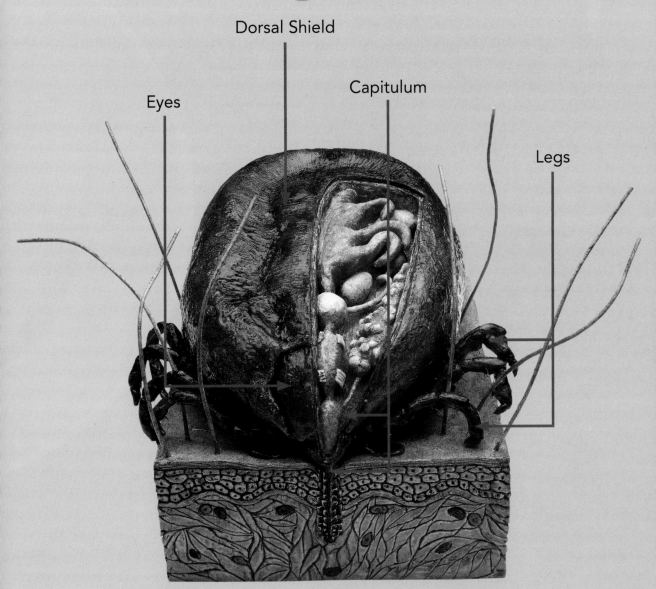

Dorsal Shield

Capitulum

Eyes

Legs

Ticks and Disease

Ticks spread diseases among animals and people. Ticks get these diseases when they feed on the blood of a sick host. The tick spreads the disease when it attaches itself to and bites a new host. Ticks can transmit many dangerous diseases.

Deer ticks carry Lyme disease. This disease has spread through most of the United States. Lyme disease has also been found in Africa, Asia, and Europe. Early signs of the disease include a rash shaped like a red bull's-eye, fever, headache, and muscle pain.

Dog ticks carry Rocky Mountain spotted fever. This disease originated in the Rocky Mountains, but it has since spread to the southern, central, and eastern regions of the United States. Rocky Mountain spotted fever causes a high fever, a skin rash, and muscle pain.

Lyme disease is the most common tick-borne disease in the **Northern Hemisphere.**

Some ticks can cause a condition called **tick paralysis**. It affects animals and young children.

Swine fever infects pigs. **Canine piroplasmosis** infects dogs. Both diseases are carried by **ticks**.

Lyme disease is named after Lyme, Connecticut. This is the town where the disease was first identified.

Most cases of **Rocky Mountain** spotted fever occur between April and September.

Ticks can also transmit babesiosis, a disease similar to **malaria**. This disease affects some animals.

Treating Bites

When an infected tick attaches to a host, the disease is not transmitted right away. Usually, a person is only infected with Lyme disease if the tick has been attached for more than 24 hours. Ticks may crawl onto people while they are walking in the woods, through tall grass, or around thick shrubs. If a tick bites, people do not usually feel anything. The only sign might be a slight redness around the bite area. Ticks often attach themselves behind the ears, on the scalp, or in places where the skin folds.

How to Remove a Tick

Anyone bitten by a tick should see a doctor. Removing a tick right away reduces the risk of disease. If far away from a medical center, people may have to remove the tick on their own. Using the tweezers, grab the tick as close to the skin as possible and pull out in one straight movement. If people twist the tick, the mouthparts may break off and stay in the skin. They could be removed separately or left until they come out as the bite wound heals. Clean your hands and the bite area with rubbing alcohol, an iodine scrub, or soap and water. You may want to save the tick in a zip-lock bag in case a doctor needs to identify the type of tick.

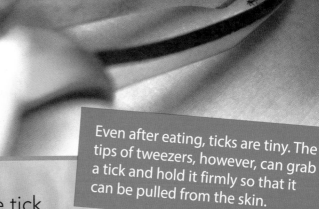

Even after eating, ticks are tiny. The tips of tweezers, however, can grab a tick and hold it firmly so that it can be pulled from the skin.

Myths and Legends

An old Navajo **folk tale** tells the story of how the wood tick got his flat shape.

Coyote lived in a tent all alone. Snow covered the ground, and Coyote was hungry. He made a wish, and when he went to the door of the tent he found a bag of deer bones. Coyote used the bones to make some soup. He ate the soup, but soon he was hungry again. Coyote made more wishes, and each time he found a bag outside the tent. Coyote knew someone was bringing him food. He had no idea who it was.

An old wizard with many arms lived nearby. He was taking food to Coyote. The next time Coyote found the food, he saw the wizard disappearing out of sight. Coyote followed the wizard to his tent on top of a hill. Coyote saw a platform where the wizard was drying deer meat. Coyote offered to carry water for the wizard if he could live there. After three days, Coyote decided to kill the wizard and keep all the meat for himself.

Coyote followed the wizard into the bushes and pounded him flat with a rock. When Coyote went back to the wizard's tent, however, all of the bones jumped up and ran away. The wizard had survived and turned the bones into live deer. As the last deer ran away, the wizard grabbed its tail and hung on. Coyote then turned the wizard into a wood tick, who would live on the deer every spring.

Charting a Tick Food Chain

Although ticks feed on other animals and are considered pests, they are part of one or more food chains. This makes them important to the environment. In this activity, create a chart that shows a tick food chain.

Materials you will need:

Two sheets of paper

Pencil

Activity

1 Using the library and the Internet, research which animals and insects eat ticks.

2 Next, create a chart that lists the animals and insects that eat ticks.

3 Beside each animal or insect, write how many ticks it eats each day.

4 On the second sheet of paper, write a paragraph describing your conclusion about how important, or unimportant, ticks are to the environment.

5 Now, draw a food chain based on the chart you created.

Know Your Stuff

Use the book to answer these questions about ticks.

1 What can a person use to remove a tick?

2 What is a hypostome?

3 What are the stages of a tick's life cycle?

4 What disease does the deer tick carry?

5 Which part of a tick's body contains the head and mouthparts?

6 How many eggs does a tick lay?

7 How many species of ticks are there?

8 What are the three main tick groups?

9 What is another name for the deer tick?

10 What is Haller's Organ?

Answers:
1. Tweezers **2.** A barbed, needle-like feeding tube inserted into the skin of the host **3.** Egg, larva, nymph, and adult **4.** Lyme disease **5.** The capitulum **6.** Between 2,000 and 18,000 **7.** More than 800 **8.** Ixodids, Argasids, and Nuttalliella **9.** The blacklegged tick **10.** A sensory organ on a tick's front legs

22

Key Words

capitulum: part of a tick's body that includes the tick's head and mouthparts

chelicerae: fanglike appendages near a tick's mouth

ecosystem: a community of all the living things and the surroundings in which they live

folk tale: a traditional story handed down over time

food chain: a group of living things that depend on each other for food

habitats: the places and surroundings where a plant or an animal lives

host: the animal or plant on which or in which another organism lives

idiosoma: part of a tick's body that includes legs, digestive stem, and reproductive organs

metamorphosis: a process during which an animal changes from one stage of development to another stage, or into an adult

molts: sheds the covering of the body

nymph: the larval form of certain insects; the third stage of the tick's life cycle

palps: part of the tick's mouth that helps the tick choose the exact spot where it will pierce its host's skin

parasites: animals or plants that live in or on others from which they obtain nourishment

scutum: the shell of a hard tick

species: a group of animals or plants that have many things in common

Index

Log on to www.av2books.com

AV² by Weigl brings you media enhanced books that support active learning. Go to www.av2books.com, and enter the special code found on page 2 of this book. You will gain access to enriched and enhanced content that supplements and complements this book. Content includes video, audio, weblinks, quizzes, a slide show, and activities.

AV² Online Navigation

Audio
Listen to sections of the book read aloud.

Video
Watch informative video clips.

Embedded Weblinks
Gain additional information for research.

Try This!
Complete activities and hands-on experiments.

Book Pages
AV² pages directly correspond to pages in the book.

Key Words
Study vocabulary, and complete a matching word activity.

Quizzes
Test your knowledge.

Slide Show
View images and captions, and prepare a presentation.

AV² was built to bridge the gap between print and digital. We encourage you to tell us what you like and what you want to see in the future.

Sign up to be an AV² Ambassador at www.av2books.com/ambassador.

Due to the dynamic nature of the Internet, some of the URLs and activities provided as part of AV² by Weigl may have changed or ceased to exist. AV² by Weigl accepts no responsibility for any such changes. All media enhanced books are regularly monitored to update addresses and sites in a timely manner. Contact AV² by Weigl at 1-866-649-3445 or av2books@weigl.com with any questions, comments, or feedback.